THE SIGN MAZE

Approaches to the Development of Signs, Labels, Markings and Instruction Manuals

Thomas F. Bresnahan, *CSP*
Donald C. Lhotka, *CSP*
Harry Winchell, *P.E., CSP*

THE SIGN MAZE

Approaches to the Development of Signs, Labels, Markings and Instruction Manuals

Published 1993 by the American Society of Safety Engineers

LIBRARY OF CONGRESS CATALOGING-IN-PUBLICATION DATA
Bresnahan, Thomas F., 1929-
    The sign maze : approaches to the development of signs, labels,
markings, and instruction manuals / Thomas F. Bresnahan, Donald C.
Lhotka, Harry Winchell.
        p.   cm.
    Includes bibliographical references and index.
    ISBN 0-939874-94-6 : $21.00
    1. Safety signs—Standards—United States.   2. Risk
communication.
I. Lhotka, Donald C., 1935-   .   II. Winchell, Harry, 1926-
III. Title.
T55.3.P67B74   1993
620.8'6—dc20   93-30075
                                              CIP

The information contained herein is not intended to be nor should it be
construed as an endorsement of a particular method or practice in sign
design and/or placement.

Printed in the United States of America

97 96 95 94 93   5 4 3 2 1

Preface

This book is for all those who either regularly, or even occasionally, must decide what goes into a sign, label, marking or instruction manual. This may be anyone whose duties include safety and health, which might include purchasing, insurance, or human resources. Architects, interior designers, building or line supervisors, product engineers, attorneys, graphic sign designers, or others in the galaxy of individuals concerned in some way with safety and health may be called upon to provide the additional service of a signage expert.

If one uses signs or labels/markings, either in the workplace or on a product, it is essential to illustrate and explain how signs interact with consumer information and employee training. Including guidance for instruction manuals in this book was therefore deemed essential. Instruction manuals can provide a complementary approach when it is necessary to call out hazard avoidance in a more tutorial manner, rather than the terse, concise, and succinct language of the sign. For these reasons, information on the use and placement of signs in instruction manuals has been provided.

In writing this book the authors had a singular purpose: to create a work which went beyond the mere narrative of what constitutes a sign, label, or marking, and to offer insights into the choices available to anyone designing a sign or even ordering or purchasing one. There may be times when the authors presume readers have a certain basic and fundamental understanding of sign usage. However, the authors have attempted to provide sufficient references which will permit most readers to delve into these subjects as their interests or job requirements dictate. The authors hope that this book becomes a valuable reference, providing direction and insight into the correct choices and decisions for those creating, purchasing or placing signs, labels, and markings.

Table of Contents

Preface

INTRODUCTION

The use of signs or markings to advise or guide people in their endeavors dates to earliest recorded history. In modern times, need for a quick and effective communications system resulted in the evolution of traffic control signs and markings on our nation's streets and highways. These devices use basic shapes, colors, and simple messages (words and pictorials) to help efficiently and safely move vehicular traffic over billions of miles each year.

This book was written because the authors believed there was considerable confusion in the minds of many safety and health professionals about what constitutes a proper sign, label or marking. Many people mistakenly feel that all signs are warnings, and, conversely, all warnings are signs. A sign listing the proper floor load of a building is simply advisory. An audible backup warning on a construction vehicle is not a sign. The rest of THE SIGN MAZE will reenforce this basic point.

The perspective on non-vehicular signs, labels and markings offered, should provide a clearer understanding of the complexity of good sign communication. Using simple advisories or directives, the basic elements of signs, labels and markings are explained. Potential problems and approaches to fostering effective communications are also discussed. A perspective on the role of litigation in the creation of adequate warnings for users of products, processes, practices, methods and systems is also offered. In addition, efforts to standardize signs/labels/markings for universal application are reviewed.

Next, an analysis and evaluation of various issues relating to current practices and uses of signs, labels, markings and instruction manuals—the "how, when, why, and where" is presented. Because attempts to standardize signs, labels, and markings have played a significant role in the evolution of these devices, a detailed discussion of this phase of their usage is provided.

Two chapters discuss the roles of research and court case review. From the subsequent discussion of research, it becomes clear why it is necessary to conduct research, and whom might be expected to assume responsibility. The chapter on legal ramifications explores the varied response of the legal system in addressing the use of signs, labels, markings and instruction manuals.

The next two chapters cover current practices and usage of signs, labels, and markings and discuss some of the more realistic considerations for the development of such devices. The current and past attempts at design and use, as well as some of the development pitfalls that can be avoided are then considered.

Instruction manuals are then reviewed, detailing basic elements that should be included in what are often a complement to signs. This chapter provides sound guidelines on how to construct a manual and how to provide proper warnings in manuals.

The Appendix contains guidelines presented to assist those developing an in-house sign standard—authored by those who have successfully negotiated the maze on several occasions. The References list other sources of information for anyone who wants to become more familiar with specific topics. There is also a glossary of terms used in this specialized field.

EXPLORING THE PROBLEMS OF SIGNS

To understand the importance of signs, labels, markings, and instruction manuals, it is essential to know where these devices fit in the hierarchy of safety efforts.

A safety hierarchy is considered to be a body of priorities or actions listed in descending order of priority. Barnett and Brinkman have pointed out,

> ...there is no such thing as *the* safety hierarchy; there are many hierarchies. Secondly "it" is not a scientific law but rather a useful rule of thumb whose genesis is consensus.[1]

In their article Barnett and Brinkman produced a table depicting what is called the "current consensus" which was determined from the available literature. The following is adopted from their table:

- First Priority—eliminate the hazard and/or risk
- Second Priority—apply safeguarding technology
- Third Priority—use warning signs
- Fourth Priority—train and instruct
- Fifth Priority—prescribe personal protection.

From the above, the importance of "warnings" as the third action (priority) in the hierarchy is readily understandable.

Signs, labels, markings and instruction manuals are used to promote safety and health by modifying and guiding human behavior. The objective is to eliminate or reduce the frequency and severity of bodily injuries and to mitigate property loss. Signs, labels, markings and instruction manuals are perhaps best described as communication devices that advise or point out a hazard to an individual.

Through years of general usage in a variety of settings, these devices have come to be regarded as warnings more than advisories or directives. *Webster's Dictionary*[2] says, in its list of synonyms under the word "advise," that "*advise* implies the making of recommendations as to a course of action...", and that "...to *caution* is to give advice that puts one on guard against possible danger, failure, etc." It further states that "*warn,* often interchangeable with caution, is used when a serious danger or penalty is involved." The authors' insertion of italics is to emphasize the circuitous nature of definitions. These definitions will also enter into the discussion of "signal words" (DANGER, WARNING, CAUTION) presented in Chapters 3, 6, and 7, and the categories or classifications of signs, etc.

The problem in describing signs,* is that not all these communication devices are used for warnings. To illustrate, consider the development, beginning in the early part of this century, of traffic control devices (signs, markings, etc.) for motor vehicle driver communication on streets and highways. The principal objective of these devices was to facilitate vehicular and pedestrian movement in a safe and efficient manner. The speed limit sign, which ultimately became standardized as rectangular with a black message on a white background, was devised as a control measure based on several criteria, not the least of which were engineering studies of the speed at which the majority of users travelled a particular section of road. The speed limit sign may be thought of as an "advisory message" which, when given the force of law, became the "warning" sign we know today.

Just as there were and still are various reasons for the way traffic control devices (signs and markings) developed, there are a variety of reasons or issues behind the development and use of any sign, label, marking, or instruction manual

There are two basic reasons or "issues" that bear upon the development and use of signs. These are external and internal by nature. External issues are those related to the effectiveness or adequacy of the message (user understanding), the need to protect the user, and requirements for providing warnings. An example of such requirements are regulations established by federal, state, or local governments to protect the safety and health of workers or

---

*Unless otherwise specified, the word "sign" used in the remainder of this book will refer collectively to signs, labels, and markings.

consumers. Internal issues are those related to designing a uniform approach for near universal application—also known as standardization—and how to reach a specific audience. An example would be workers in a special industry such as nuclear power or telecommunications.

ADEQUACY OF WARNINGS

There has been and will continue to be considerable debate as to what constitutes an adequate warning.

Warnings are intended to assure safe use of products, processes, practices, or systems where hazards exist. Warnings are justified based on the stated degree of hazard; and, of course, when the consequences and avoidance action are not obvious to a reasonably competent person, such guidance should also be given. Emphasis on the adequacy of the sign becomes essential, if one understands that a sign or decal on a machine is not an adequate alternative to eliminating hazards by design or providing proper guarding on a machine. (Remember to refer to the safety hierarchy.)

The purpose of visual (signs) warnings is to call attention to a hazard and to change or reinforce the way it will be perceived by the viewer in order to avoid accidents or injuries. Generally, a warning is desirable when a hazard is foreseeable, in addition to meeting the following criteria:

(1) The hazard is, by definition, dangerous;
(2) The danger poised by the hazard is or should be known to the producer, manufacturer, supplier, or facility manager;
(3) The danger is not one which is obvious, known, or readily discoverable by the user (viewer);
(4) The danger is not one which arises because the product or substance is put to some completely irrational use by a viewer.

The warning must also extend to all individuals who may be reasonably expected to encounter the hazard. This includes workers, consumers, and even casual guests within a facility.

STANDARDIZATION

An issue of significant importance in sign development is the need for universal criteria, more commonly known as standardization. A good description of one purpose of standardization can be found in a guide of the International Organization for Standardization[3] which deals with the treatment of safety in the preparation of standards:

> In standardization, the safety of products, processes and services is generally considered with a view to achieving the optimum balance between a number of factors, including non-technical factors such as human behavior, that will eliminate avoidable risks of harm to persons and goods to an acceptable level ("level of safety").

Of course, standardization is an internal issue. It is internal because the effectiveness of the sign to communicate its message comes from the criteria needed to address all the parameters that make up the sign; that is, shape, color, size, readability, configuration, etc. Standardization is essential to avoid confusion in communicating a desired action, but it is also essential in obtaining quick, almost programmable response to the message. If it takes three to four minutes to think about a sign's message, it obviously does not meet the intended objective—to communicate a message quickly.

Instruction manuals seemingly deviate from this principle of behavior modification in a fundamental way. However, instruction manuals should have certain approaches which are designed to avoid confusion and to facilitate broader and more fundamental understanding. More will be presented later in a detailed review of instruction manuals.

To the casual observer, standardization of signs would appear to be an uncomplicated endeavor. After all, aren't highway traffic control signs a good example of simple shapes, colors, pictorials, or words that are almost internationally recognized? Anyone old enough to remember or who has studied the field of traffic control can attest to the fact that traffic signs did not become standardized "overnight." In the beginning, almost every state, county, city or hamlet had its own way of controlling vehicular and pedestrian movement. The establishment of a federal agency (the old Bureau of Public Roads) and, later, the development of the federal Interstate Defense Highway System led to the standardization of traffic signs, four of which are shown in Figure 1.

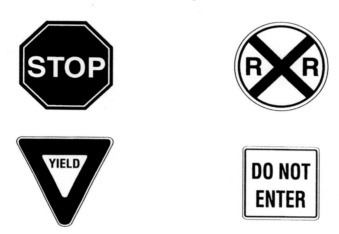

Figure 1. Four standard U.S. traffic signs.

In order to understand the factors involved in the approach to development of a sign system, a comparison of highway with nonvehicle signage is, once again, instructive. Highway transportation agencies eventually realized that establishing uniform interstate highway traffic signs facilitated recognition and comprehension. In addition, it was found that standardization increased the ease with which viewer training can be implemented and obtained.

Just as highway sign recognition and comprehension are bolstered and re-enforced by license testing, training can also be used in the workplace to achieve better recognition and then improve reaction time to a hazard. However, many product labels or warning signs are not easily recognized by the viewer.

The full benefits of standardization are often not immediately realized. A good example is the length of time it took for the U.S. Forest Service to get "Smokey Bear" recognized as a symbol of forest fire prevention—an estimated twenty years.

Standardization of signs in the workplace or environment (public buildings or areas) for years had been a matter of jurisdiction, usually a federal, state, or local agency. Signs in relation to products were usually standardized within an industry or possibly not at all. Since the early 1960s, however, the need for standard and consistent signs has generated a great deal of debate and discussion throughout the United States and the world.

DEVELOPMENT AND HISTORY OF SIGN STANDARDIZATION

THE 1941 STANDARD

Accident prevention signs have probably been used for a longer period of time than any other item of safety equipment. That constructive thought has previously been given to accident prevention signs is shown by the following paragraph take from Signs and Slogans, a booklet published by the Independence Inspection Bureau in 1914, which was referenced in the American National Standard Z35.1-1941 (R-1945):

> You can't always apply mechanical safeguards. Nor can you be present always to caution men of danger. Signs will help you. Use substantial signs—place them properly—and maintain them in good condition.

One of the leading organizations involved in sign standardization has been the American National Standards Institute (ANSI), formerly known as the American Standards Association. Through the years, this organization has been responsible for the promulgation of numerous national standards including those related to safety in general and safety signs specifically.

In another booklet, *Universal Safety Standards,* also published in 1914, there appeared a section "Standards for Danger and Safety Signs" which basically was much the same as the first ANSI, then ASA, standard. Work on these sign standards began in 1935 and culminated in 1941 when the initial standard was printed.

The following, excerpted from the Introduction to the American Standard Z35.1-1941, "Specifications for Industrial Accident Prevention Signs," sums up the thinking of the time and the need for a sign standard:

> Sign uniformity is of great importance. When various concerns in either the same or different industries all

> use signs of definite design and color to warn of par-
> ticular hazard, to express caution, [Authors' emphasis]
> to provide general information, or to point out direc-
> tions, the use of accident prevention signs will be con-
> siderably more effective. Such practice will result in
> workers becoming familiar with the few necessary
> sign designs, no matter where they work, and confu-
> sion with unfamiliar signs will be avoided.[1]

There are still good reasons for sign standards even in the face
of thoughtful, well intended articles, such as M. G. Moore's[2] which
question the efficacy of such standards.

The original Scope and Purpose of American Standard Z35.1-
1941 gives an excellent indication of how broadly the standard
might be applied. It stated, in part:

> These specifications apply to design, application, and
> use of signs or symbols...intended to indicate and,
> insofar as possible, to define specific hazards of a
> nature such that failure to designate them may lead to
> accidental injury to workers, or the public, or both.

The drafters of the standard obviously saw an impact of signs
on persons other than only those in the workplace environment.
(An example of a sign warning about a wet floor probably best
illustrates what they had in mind.) In addition, the above statement of application foresaw and provided for the possibility of
members of the public (visitors) being found in a workplace facility
or the signs being used in public places, or for other purposes,
such as on products.

Another interesting aspect of the original Standard was that it
was not exclusionary as far as personal injury and property damage accidents were concerned. The current standards, the Z535
series, focus almost exclusively upon personal injury without any
reference to hazards capable of causing a combination of injury
and property damage. Such an approach seems to be a fallacious
view of accident causation where it eliminates from the standard
the majority of accidents/incidents which can produce both personal injury and property damage. This "either or" method
restricts the sign producer to accident scenarios which do not
track with accident data or experiences. Adding to the unwarranted limiting of the current standards are the definitions of

signs which do not allow application of the standards to hazards leading to personal injury and/or property damage.* (See Appendix A.)

A very significant part of the 1941 standard, now superseded, as it relates to current efforts, was Section 4, "Sign Purposes," which stated:

> Uniformity shall be maintained for the following purposes:
> (a) Danger signs—to warn of specific dangers only.
> (b) Caution signs—to warn of possible dangers or unsafe practices.
> (c) Safety Instruction signs—to provide information relating to general safe practices.
> (d) Directional signs—to indicate the way to stairways, fire escapes, exits, and other locations.
> (e) Informational signs—to carry messages of a general nature, such as rules, regulations, and markers, when such postings do not conflict with Danger or Caution purposes.

These "classifications," illustrated in Figure 2, are an important element of sign development which will be further detailed and explained in the "Signal Words" section in the next chapter.

Change of Classes and Definitions

For thirty years (1941-1971), these sign classifications remained relatively intact through five revisions. In the 1970s, the Z35.1-1972 Standard[3] adopted a change of classes and their definitions. The first two classes were still known as DANGER and CAUTION, which literally formed the basis of a two-level hazardous alerting system. However, the last three classes became known as General Safety, Fire and Emergency, and Radiation. To delineate more precisely the two levels of hazards, a supplemental Standard known as Z35.4-1973, "Specifications for Informational Signs Complementary to ANSI Z35.1-1972, Accident Prevention Signs"[4] was created to encompass the last three classes of signs which were informational in nature.

---

*The Z535.2 and Z535.4 Standards do recognize the potential property damage in the footnotes, as if an afterthought.

Figure 2. Illustrations of different sign classifications.

The significance of creating the Z35.1 and Z35.4 standards was to preserve the two-tier or two-level hazard association values (HAVs) for only precautionary warning signs. By breaking out and separating the general safety information signs (NOTICE and SAFETY FIRST), a limit was set corresponding to the causation of accident/injury being either immediate (DANGER) or random (CAUTION). This division, found in the 1968 (later superseded) edition of the Z35.1 standard, should not be seen as a rationale for creating another or second visual system based upon where the sign is located on a product, in the environment, part of a system or method, or any other contingency of location.

In short, a sign is a communication whose elements or factors are stereotyped by human factors experiments to determine what the viewer/perceiver sees in the sign. Where it is located or how it is applied (e.g., tags wired to a fixture) is not the critical test for what goes into the sign.

OTHER STANDARDS

Over the years, the need for standardization of signs became well recognized by various industries and many of the specifications for such signs were published as American National Standards. Some ANSI Standards addressing other subjects, include detailed and abbreviated guidelines on applicable safety signs, labels, and instruction manuals. One is ANSI Z129.1-1988, "Precautionary Labeling of Hazardous Industrial Chemicals."[5] Others were published by professional organizations such as the American Society of Agricultural Engineers and the Society of Automotive Engineers. Figure 3 shows four of these symbols.

American National Standard Radiation Symbol, N2.1-1988

 American National Standard Biological Hazard Symbol, originally in Z35.5

 American Society of Agricultural Engineers (ANSI/ASAE) S350, Safety-Alert Symbol for Agricultural Equipment

 American Society of Agricultural Engineers (ANSI/ASAE) S276.3, Slow Moving Vehicle Identification Emblem

Figure 3. Symbols developed by ANSI and ASAE.

One major factor for continuing efforts to standardize signs has been the establishment of regulations under the federal Consumer Product Safety Commission (CPSC) and the Occupational Safety and Health Administration (OSHA). OSHA standards, using the national consensus standards of ANSI and NFPA, contain minimum recommendations for signs, tags, labels, markings, etc., to meet the duty of an employer to adequately warn employees of hazards, dangerous conditions, or situations. For example, the OSHA Code of Federal Regulations 1910.145 establishes rules for signs and tags, and CFR 1910.1200 (Hazard Communication) provides for information on labels and other forms of warnings to alert employees to the presence of hazardous chemicals and how to handle them.

OTHER FACTORS FOR STANDARDIZATION

Aside from federal regulation of workplace signs, a significant incentive for standardization has come from what became known as the "product liability revolution" of the 1970s. Some observers point to the early 1960s as the beginning of the revolution in which judicial involvement "directed" manufacturers as to their role in guiding consumers in the safe usage of their products, as well as to warning consumers against improper usage.

The primary reason for the involvement of the courts was, of course, the large increase in product liability litigation in the 1960s and '70s, and the subsequent increases in assessments of damages against the manufacturers involved. Whereas a million-dollar verdict against a product maker was very rare before 1970, during the next decade these verdicts became comparatively commonplace. The machine tool, automotive, and chemicals industries, among others, found that they had a large stake in properly designed and standardized warnings. Their trade associations and professional organizations spent considerable time and effort providing guidance and recommendations for handling problems related to the use of adequate warnings. They also mounted extensive public education efforts through meetings, seminars, and public services announcements to get the message to their constituents.

The growing number of cases alleging inadequacies in the effectiveness of warnings to consumers did stimulate a re-evaluation of sign design and development among many interested and affected organizations and individual manufacturers.

The reaction to these events produced differing opinions as to what constituted proper warnings within specific industries. Each industry approached the problem from different perspectives based on differing experiences in court, or preconceived impressions about how consumers would accept warnings, or a number of other reasons. During the 1970s, major corporations developed their own greatly varied systems for signs/labels/markings. These sign systems were primarily designed as a response to the impact of the "product liability revolution."

CURRENT AMERICAN NATIONAL STANDARD DEVELOPMENT

In the late 1970s the newly accredited Z535 Standards Committee began the revision of the previous Z35 Sign Standards Series and the Z53 Standard, "Safety Color Code for Marking Physical Hazards,"[6] under the title ANSI Z535, "Safety Signs and Colors." The scope statement contained in the 1972 Standard (Z35.1, "Accident Prevention Signs") applied to personal injury, property damage, or both situations. Historically, previous ANSI Sign Standards were concerned with public and workplace safety signs which were interpreted to apply to products. Illustrative of this interpretation is the use of the Z35 sign system in the ANSI A14 Ladder, A92 Elevating Work Platforms, B20 Conveyers, and other product-related standards.

The Z535 Committee has put together a series of separate standards, approved in June, 1991,[7] which cover the following:

Z535.1 Safety Color Code
Z535.2 Environmental and Facility Signs
Z535.3 Criteria for Safety Symbols
Z535.4 Product Safety Signs and Labels
Z535.5 Accident Prevention Tags

Unfortunately, two standards (Environmental/Facility Signs and Product Signs) attempt to create and apply what appears to be different sets of requirements to the task of designing or selecting signs.

The principal concern these standards address is that safety signs and product signs/labels appear to have distinctly different users and applications. Environmental and workplace signs are usually larger, observed from longer distances, and often contained fewer details, which increases visual clarity. Product signs or labels are likely to: have more information in a smaller layout; observed at close range; be available for a wide range of product sizes and shapes; and should contrast (stand out) with the color of the product to which they are affixed.

Upon close examination, the position posited by the standards concerning the differences in environmental and product signs seems shallow, perhaps even unsound, when the facts are considered. The requirement that one sign be larger than another ignores the nature of the hazard, which ultimately will determine or dictate the message's content.

The nature of the hazard also dictates the size of the sign within the parameters of clarity and the absence of word clutter and visual noise. Clarity rather than clutter is an absolute for any sign. The real issue in sign design is the need to provide the necessary information which will alert everyone who is impacted by specific hazards, whether the hazard is in the environment, related to a product, or identified by a tag. The factors used to differentiate between signs based upon location rather than viewer capabilities appear artificial, and do not take into account how a sign is designed for specific placement in relation to a hazard or group of hazards.

As indicated above, the current Z535 series of standards call for two separate sign standards—one for environmental facilities and another for products. Obviating the need for two such systems of signs are the commonalities that exist in both. Each uses a three-level hazardous alerting values (HAVs) system, the same safety colors and signal words, and the same definitions.

The three-level system uses the signal words "DANGER", "WARNING", and "CAUTION". The definitions of these signal words strictly position them in descending order of risk according to the level of potential bodily injury. Z535.2 and Z535.4 make it clear that "DANGER" and "WARNING" signal words are not to be used for situations which might involve property damage accidents, unless personal injury risk consistent with these levels is also involved. They do allow "CAUTION" (and "NOTICE") to be used for property-damage-only accident/hazards.

The issue involves the significance of the HAV of "CAUTION" or "NOTICE" in certain circumstances. For example, if an expensive machine fails because of an inappropriate action which was warned by a "CAUTION" sign and an entire plant is closed, was the HAV of the sign sufficient?

There are various views on the merits of these standards. Some industries and organizations view the three-level HAVs as unrealistic in the way accidents occur. For this reason, they believe that it is more appropriate to have a two-tier sign system. However, discussion of the advantages of a 2-tier versus a 3-tier sign system must recognize that:

- Definitions of signal words such as "will," "could," and "may," are subjective and non-quantitative in nature. This subjective use of words is not consistent with appropriate standards writing technique.

- The apparent lack of attention to property damage hazard communication makes it difficult to choose signal words. This is in spite of the fact that the definition of the word "accident" has a property damage component as well as bodily injury aspects.

- Two sign systems (Z535.2 and Z535.4) might induce product manufacturers who are also employers to have disparate signs, e.g. one for product and one for environment.

- Two standards (Z535.2 and Z535.4) are duplicative and create an unnecessary second graphic system for signs.

- Specifications in the standards are not "user friendly" because of the difficulty in understanding conflicting restrictions.

Some industries have, through experience or legal encounters, settled on their own designs and are fearful that changes required through dual national sign standards would be difficult to uphold if challenged in court. (For guidance in considering a uniform sign design approach see the Appendix.)

THE ROLE OF RESEARCH IN DEVELOPING SIGNS

In the past 10 to 15 years, there have been almost countless formal studies conducted and results published on various aspects of sign research.* These studies can be very helpful to sign designers, especially where new situations demand that a sign be tested. This is particularly true when "different" pictorials or words/phrases are used.

An indication of the ambiguity concerning sign design and employers'/manufacturers' "duty to warn" was that in one organization it was recommended that the word "WARNING" be inserted in the red oval of the traditional "DANGER" sign as well as the upper panel of the "CAUTION" sign. This action may seem amusing, but it is indicative of the climate in which an almost one-dimensional legal orientation can be applied to corporate decision making. To present the best recommendations on the subject of labeling, marking, placarding, signing, or more simply called "duty to warn," guidelines other than those found in the law or provided by research must be consulted.

The most currently definitive and precise of these guidelines, *WARNINGS—Guiding Principles,* is a compilation of 17 criteria provided by a major insurance company to the American National Standards Institute Committee ANSI A92, "Elevated Work Platforms." Of particular note among these 17 criteria is No. 9, which states:

> In the preparation of warnings, have there been preliminary safety analyses to discover what the hazards might be and are there any human factors engineering evaluations as to how best to communicate with the user through labels, warnings, cautions, brochures, pamphlets, manual, and instruction?[1]

---

*An excellent reference is *Instructions and Warnings: The Annotated Bibliography* by Mark R. Lehto, James M. Miller, and Paul J. Frantz (Ann Arbor: Fuller Technical Publications, 1990).

Surprisingly, several organizations and standards committees have adopted the approach of developing such human factors engineering evaluations and applied research as guides to developing their signs and labels. For example, one ovenware manufacturer actually field tested product misuse warnings with its intended audience. In another instance an American National Standards committee used its own statistical injury data and plugged it into the findings of sign research to develop a labeling/marking system for its product standard (A14 Standards Rationale Statement).[2] (Figure 4 shows a sample label developed based on the A14 Statement.)

Data collected from such evaluations provide for the more effective design of precautions, dangers, warnings, and safety instructions. The use of such data should be axiomatic in the development of standards which might change the design of signs, labels, or markings. Without sufficient human factor engineering evaluations, potential injury and maybe even catastrophe are possible. A classic example of human factors evaluations to avert catastrophe is provided by Collins and Lerner[3] in which Fire Symbols were studied. The study revealed problems in the comprehension of "EXIT" and "No-EXIT" symbols. One can only speculate about the consequences of evacuating people to a "No-EXIT" area in a fire and smoke filled building where precious time would be lost in back-tracking to an exit. It is not enough to simply mandate a sign or symbol. Thorough evaluation must be conducted.

Sign/label testing is important from a product safety point of view (although not always required). If a manufacturer is able to document the effectiveness of a product sign/label, an essential part of a legal defense is established against claims of product defect because of the failure to warn. On the other hand, workplace facility signs also should be tested not only for effectiveness, but also for clarity, visibility (lighting), and for placement. A hidden sign does little to help avoid serious problems.

If an individual sign designer does not feel comfortable in planning a test for her/his work, there are several competent research organizations (such as the Human Factors Society) which can be used. Costs for such work vary from a few hundred dollars for simple evaluations of color choice and sign shape to hundreds of thousands for elaborate evaluations of perception, warning impact, and sign effectiveness. Several trade associations and standards committees have, as just mentioned, adopted approaches to

Figure 4. Example of a ladder label based on data compiled by the American National Standard A14 Committee.

sign/label/marking development which utilize human factors engineering evaluations and applied research as guides, including testing protocols.

Formal research tends to address the broader aspects of sign/label/marking design. A number of researchers have looked at warning effectiveness; user/viewers perceptions of color, pictorials, shape, etc.; and, signal word identification and response. Studies conducted thus far usually support the contention that a conspicuously designed and placed warning sign/label will influence readers/users to behave cautiously. Unfortunately, not very many studies have involved behavioral research where people were actually using products or processes in a work environment when the evaluations were made. Most have been done in academic settings, using graduate or undergraduate students as subjects. Studies, such as those conducted by Lehto, Miller and Frantz can be useful as models for effective research.

Empirical or practical research on sign/label effectiveness has generally been confined to individual employers, manufacturers, and technical groups. These studies are more practical because they almost always try to reach the actual viewers/users of products, processes, or systems. It is not unusual for a sign designer to approach the affected viewers of a hazardous situation to measure the effectiveness or a warning of misuse or unsafe behavior. This often occurs when a claim for damages is made citing a peculiar misuse or specific incident, perhaps one not even considered feasible by the designer. As a matter of fact, experience has proven that it is a good idea to use consumer/user complaints or claims, association membership experiences, complaints to government agencies, or similar vehicles to learn of problems with various communications devices. An example of this is the action taken by the A14 Ladder Standards Committee to improve labels on portable ladders. The committee relied on information generated through the ANSI Consumer Sounding Boards across the U.S.

A useful technique to get information of sign/label/marking significance in any accident incident is to use a feedback report form. Similar forms can be used for products where a sales or field representative staff can be involved. An example of this type of survey form is illustrated in Figure 5.

Feedback Survey

In your last accident/injury report was a sign/label or other precautionary marking used to try to prevent the accidental occurrence?

☐ YES   ☐ NO

If you answered YES:

A. Did the occurrence involve:
   - ☐ Injury only
   - ☐ Property damage
   - ☐ Both above items

B. Was the sign mounted on a:
   - ☐ Product/machine/device
   - ☐ Plant wall/pillar/dock
   - ☐ Tag fastened to above items

C. Was sign posting required by a/an:
   - ☐ OSHA regulation
   - ☐ Building code
   - ☐ National Standard (ANSI/NFPA)
   - ☐ Industry standard
   - ☐ Accepted good safety practice

D. Was the sign visible (not obscured)?
   ☐ YES   ☐ NO

E. Could the sign have been placed more prominently?
   ☐ YES   ☐ NO

F. Did presence of other signs distract to confuse the viewer?
   ☐ YES   ☐ NO

G. Was the sign large enough—letters and overall size?
   ☐ YES   ☐ NO

H. Did general and natural lighting illuminate the sign enough?
   ☐ YES   ☐ NO

I. Was the sign understood?
   ☐ YES   ☐ NO
   1. Should it have been in another language?
      ☐ YES   ☐ NO

J. Did the sign alert soon enough to avoid incident?
   ☐ YES   ☐ NO

K. Was the hazard obvious?
   ☐ YES   ☐ NO

L. Does job training include sign recognition and understanding signs?
   ☐ YES   ☐ NO

M. Was the sign one of the following types?
   - ☐ DANGER   ☐ CAUTION
   - ☐ NOTICE   ☐ SAFETY FIRST
   - ☐ OTHER

1. Were symbols used?
   ☐ YES   ☐ NO

2. Did the other words on the sign:
   a. Tell what hazard was?
      ☐ YES   ☐ NO
   b. Tell how to avoid hazard?
      ☐ YES   ☐ NO
   c. Tell what would happen if not avoided?
      ☐ YES   ☐ NO
   d. If b and c are NO, was hazard obvious?
      ☐ YES   ☐ NO

N. The above sign would be:
   - ☐ 1. Manufactured in house
   - ☐ 2. Ordered from catalog

   If from catalog would type and wording of sign have been specified?
   ☐ YES   ☐ NO   ☐ MAYBE

If you answered NO:

a. Have you seen near-misses here?
   ☐ YES   ☐ NO

b. Would a sign have been helpful to avoid the accidental occurrence?
   ☐ YES   ☐ NO   ☐ MAYBE

O. What type of sign would be chosen?
   - ☐ DANGER—high hazard
   - ☐ CAUTION—mid hazard
   - ☐ SAFETY FIRST—low hazard
   - ☐ NOTICE—vital information
   - ☐ OTHER

P. Who would specify the type and wording of the sign?
   - ☐ Plant Superintendent
   - ☐ Maintenance
   - ☐ Purchasing
   - ☐ Engineering
   - ☐ Safety Committee
   - ☐ Safety Director
   - ☐ Combination of above
   - ☐ Others not listed

Q. Signs would be:
   - ☐ 1. Designed and produced in-house
   - ☐ 2. Found in catalog and ordered

Figure 5. Sample feedback survey.

5

LEGAL IMPLICATIONS

CASE LAW

As part of the process of understanding the various aspects of sign design, it is important to be aware of the legal implications of the actions taken by or omissions of a designer. The following discussion is not meant to be an exhaustive review or listing of these implications, but to illustrate some of the legal nuances that sign design can impose.

The November 1982 issue of *Professional Safety,* the official publication of the American Society of Safety Engineers, reprinted an article from *Trial Magazine*[1] written by Harry Philo, a renowned plaintiff attorney. It was an excellent compendium of legal criteria in the area of product liability "duty to warn." Mr. Philo discussed: causation, burden of proof of causation, ordinary consumer expectations, conformance to Warning Standards, and other applicable criteria.

However, such articles should not be seen as the complete word on "duty to warn," as there are aspects and approaches that are beyond such a limited view. Missing from such discussions is the entire range of human factors engineering concerned with the cognitive facilities of recognition, identification, and evaluation of warnings or safety instructions.

There are many cases cited in legal literature which cover multiple aspects of "failure to warn" relative to signs, labels, markings or instruction manuals. The cases presented in this chapter were chosen to guide a reader through the extent to which courts have applied the principle of "failure to warn," the converse of which is a manufacturer's "duty to warn." These cases generally contain additional allegations, but in this review only the salient points in the cases related to warnings and signs are presented.

Lack of Warning and Extension of Responsibility to Warn

Todalen v. U.S. Chemical Co., 424 N.W. 2d 73 Minnesota Court of Appeals 1988

An employer bought a chemical caustic from the manufacturer for cleaning purposes. Both knew of the violent reactiveness of the chemical when mixed with water; however, there was no warning of such reaction on the chemical's container. An employee poured the chemical down a clogged drain and a reaction occurred and the employee suffered severe facial burns. The results of the plaintiff and defense presentations verified that the employer's main concern in the purchase of the chemical was its cleaning ability, not the health risks to the employee. Additionally the employer could not be expected to know as much as the manufacturer did about the product; therefore, the manufacturer's duty to warn any user (through adequate labeling, etc.) was required.

Ineffective Warning

> *Aura* v. *Harris Graphics Corp.*, U.S. District Court D, Mass., No. 86-1081-S, Feb 9, 1988.

In order to clean a printing press, an employee had to remove a spring-loaded nip point guard. Originally, the press design called for a permanent guard, but it was changed to allow for cleaning. The press did have a sign which warned against operating the equipment without the guard, but the operator's manual gave no warning as to the dangers of operating the press without guards. Since the press could not be cleaned with the guard in place and it had to be operated to be cleaned, the court ruled that this made the warning ineffective.

Instruction Manual Inconsistency

> *Pingsterhaus* v. *Lear Siegler, Inc.*, St. Clair County (Ill.) Circuit Court, No. 85-L-838, May 17, 1988.

A box-shaped hopper that contained an auger was used to load feed into a bin. The hopper was located on the ground at the end of a long chute and it had a lid or cover which was open. An employee attempted to lean across the hopper to close the lid and was injured by the auger. The manufacturer claimed the auger was designed for use only on grain bin roofs. However, the plaintiff produced a manual published by the defendant which showed the use of the equipment *on the ground*. The plaintiff also alleged that the equipment failed to have any warnings on it concerning imminent dangers.

Failure to Meet Industry Labeling Standards

> *Cox* v. *C E NATCO,* Burleigh County (ND) District Court, No. 36618, March 16, 1988.

A drum, which formerly contained an oil field chemical product and flammable xylene, was sold to a neighbor of a welder who wanted to convert it to a waste container. As the welder used a cutting torch on the end of the drum it exploded. Through the discovery process, the plaintiff was able to determine that the defendant had failed to meet chemical industry labeling standards. These called for labeling of products which contained flammable liquids to warn of the need to keep such products away from heat, sparks and open flame.

Costly Delay in Warning Development

> *Perkins* v. *White Stores, Inc.,* Tarrant County (TX) 348th Judicial District Court, No. 348-72132-82, April 18, 1988.

A car battery exploded while its cables were being loosened and a person standing nearby was seriously injured. The plaintiff claimed, among other factors, the failure to adequately warn because, during the discovery process, it was determined that the battery manufacturer was working on a label warning of explosion possibilities. The manufacturer did, in fact, put such labels on batteries made one month after the exploding battery was produced.

Summary

These cases are good examples of how litigants develop, at least in part, the product or process defect known as "failure to warn." Whether the warnings are used as signs/labels or in instruction manuals, the developer of such messages should be aware of the alleged shortcomings of others and court decisions such as those presented above.

Based on court decisions, the following checklist is helpful when considering the legal implications of the effectiveness of signs or their messages.

- Clearly convey the magnitude of the dangers involved;

- Tailor the message to the level of the user's education;

- Document who receives and uses the product or process;

- Attract immediate attention;

- Use understandable words, not all technical terms or jargon;

- Use correct colors; results of litigation show a preference for "exciter colors" such as red, yellow, orange, and black;

- Consider rectangular shaped designs, bearing in mind that the oval shape is considered the least desirable;

- Do not detract from the sign message and do not leave out essential words;

- Use strong clear language easily visible in line of sight;

- Document any testing, which should be current, with end users;

- Prioritize the risks in the signs from highest to lowest;

- Consider legal implications of signal word choice.

6

CURRENT PRACTICES AND USAGE OF SIGNS, LABELS, AND

As indicated earlier, the application and use of signs as warnings has resulted in a hodgepodge of shapes, colors, pictorials and words, especially in the product safety field. Very often, the reasons given for such situations are:

- Not enough room or space available;

- Sign colors clashed with background colors;

- Use of some other signal word because "DANGER" or "WARNING" might convey severe hazard; and,

- Creative or artistic license.

Signs, in general, have identified hazards which cannot be eliminated by following accepted levels of design and safeguarding, as suggested in the "safety hierarchy." Although cautionary warnings should be in the language of the viewer of the product, process, or service, sign wording should identify the risk involved. In some instances, the message of the sign is very straight forward in describing conditions, prohibitions, or other precautions identified by the hazard, for example, "NO SMOKING", "KEEP OUT", "HARD HAT AREA", "POISON", or "EXPLOSIVES". Signing is not always so easily done, but where it threatens to become more complicated this basic simplicity should be the goal or objective.

As the process of designing a sign becomes more complex than the single word or message sign, attention must be given to structure and definition. The first element of the structure is the division of the sign into two (2) basic panels—upper and lower. In some cases, a third panel for a symbol or graphic is included. The upper panel is generally where the signal word is placed, often within a special shape or configuration; e.g., a red oval with a white border is inserted into a black background in the "DANGER" sign. This upper panel may also be used for a key word such as "EXPLOSIVES" while the lower panel might provide an admonition of "NO SMOKING". In cases of hazard avoidance, the lower panel may define the precautionary information as well as the consequences of failure to avoid the hazard. Of course, a symbol on a third panel, either to the right or left of the basic sign, can supplement the word message or be included as part of the lower panel if only a two panel sign is selected.

COLORS[1]

Although the colors red, black, and white will normally be found on signs depicting "DANGER", one can find a variety of deviations from this color scheme actually used. However, typically, red letters for "DANGER" appears on a white background or, occasionally, white letters on a red background. (See Fig. 6.)

Figure 6. Typical color designations for "DANGER" signs.

Typically, both "WARNING" and "DANGER" signs have been principally in red and white. More recently as specified in the ANSI Z535 standards, the use of "safety orange," sometimes known as "hunter's orange," has been required. Like "DANGER" signs, however, these signs also have employed various colors for a number of reasons. (See Fig. 7.)

Figure 7. Typical color designations for "WARNING" signs.

"CAUTION" sign colors are usually yellow and black. It is not unusual, however, to find the yellow letters "CAUTION" on a white background or vice versa. Different borders are also used, such as alternating colors (yellow and black) as squares or slashes. (See Fig. 8.)

Figure 8. Typical color designations for "CAUTION" signs.

Blue and white background colors, with black message lettering, are normally found on "NOTICE" signs. (See Fig. 9.)

Figure 9. Typical color designations for "NOTICE" signs.

Green and white, with black message lettering, has been preferred for "SAFETY INFORMATION" signs. (See Fig. 10.) Like other signs, variations in the colors used are not uncommon.

Figure 10. Typical color designations for "SAFETY INFORMATION" signs.

SIGNAL WORDS

The objective of the signal word portion of a sign is twofold: to indicate the level of hazard or risk exposure for an individual, and to serve as an alert or "attention getter" to show the *amount* of hazard. In the case of traffic control signs, the intended message is the signal word, such as STOP, YIELD, CURVE, SLOW, etc. This is also true of the EXIT signs used in buildings. The use of signal words for non-vehicular sign use are: DANGER, WARNING, CAUTION, NOTICE, and SAFETY FIRST.

There have been some efforts to add a recognizable symbol to signal words for quicker identification of the intent of the sign. The symbol used is an equilateral triangle with an exclamation mark in the center as specified in other standards. (Refer to Fig. 3.) This symbol has been primarily used in the agricultural industry, and more widely in Europe than in the U.S.

A better approach may be to use a symbol which reflects or is pertinent to the hazard being identified. On power presses for example, the crushing symbol for machinery hazards is more pertinent than an exclamation mark surrounded by an equilateral triangle.

A generic alerting symbol, such as the raised hand indicating "halt" or octagon "STOP" sign, which is more recognizable may be desired. Giving more credence to such an approach is a recent study by Wogalter, Jarrard, and Simpson, *Effects of Warning Signal Words on Hazard Perception of Consumer Products*[2] which calls into serious question the use of the exclamation mark in the equilateral triangle.

CONFIGURATION AND PICTORIALS

Traffic control signs rely substantially on shape to distinguish the intent of the message. The best known example is the octagon for "STOP". However, signs for environmental, product, or workplace use can be found in a variety of shapes, sizes, and layouts.

The most prevalent shape for non-traffic signs is the rectangle. Where signal words are used, they are normally found in a panel at the top of the sign and the message is below in the lower panel. Both panels comprising the sign can be squeezed or elongated vertically or horizontally to accommodate the desired location.

Pictorials are generally found as a black illustration on a white background.[3] However, depending on the class of sign and the creativity of the designer, many other combinations are in use. Typically, a pictorial should be simple and yet must convey the hazard or risk exposure precisely. Some examples of well-accepted pictorials are shown in Figure 11. Ideally, pictorials convey both the nature of the hazard and the consequences of not avoiding the hazard.

A recent study[4] reported that a potential problem may exist where the mere recognition of a pictorial (a flame symbol) could result in a false sense of security when using the product. Seeing the symbol of the flame, a user/viewer might conclude that the product itself, an adhesive, was flammable and not recognize that it is the vapors which represent the real hazard. The study concluded that "...the presence of one symbol on a product can influence the interpretation of other symbols as well as the warning text on the label...". It further stressed "...evaluation of symbol interpretation and effectiveness will need to be conducted in the context of the entire label rather than testing the symbol in isolation...". The point is that generic symbols should not be employed unless tested or evaluated in specific context with the purpose of the overall message.

Figure 11. Some examples of well-developed pictorials.

THE MESSAGE MAZE

Messages on signs are as varied as there are ideas that arise to create them. This situation is not necessarily bad, unless the message contains language not specific to a particular industry. As the original Z35.1-1941 standard scope statement reported, the concept of uniformity in signs (and their messages) is most desirable to assist workers in industries, particularly where movement from facility to facility is common. A classic example of such transient workers is in the construction trades.

Generally, the message format includes the signal word, typography (printed words) and a pictorial. A common problem observed in signage is "the more words or instructions used the less space available for pictorials and signal words." In some cases, a pictorial may not be feasible. For example, where a sign reads:

```
┌─────────────────────────────────┐
│                                 │
│      CANCER SUSPECT AGENT       │
│    AUTHORIZED PERSONNEL ONLY     │
│                                 │
└─────────────────────────────────┘
```

it would be difficult to conceive of an appropriate pictorial. As indicated earlier, part of the reason for using pictorials is quicker recognition of a hazard and another is the problem of understanding the printed word. In some areas, literacy and choice of language can pose problems for the sign designer.

Some sign messages try to be all-encompassing to meet legal criteria, marketing needs, and engineering design. These will undoubtedly lead to greater confusion rather than getting the message across. An example of a complicated, somewhat confusing label is shown in Figure 12.

CAUTION

CONTAINS

PCBs

(Polychlorinated Biphenyls)

A toxic environmental contaminant requiring special handling and disposal in accordance with U.S. Environmental Protection Agency Regulations 40 CFR 761—For Disposal Information contact the nearest U.S. E.P.A. Office.

In Case of accident or spill, call toll free the U.S. Coast Guard National Response Center. 800:424-8802

Also Contact _____

Tel. No. _____

Figure 12. An example of a label which might cause confusion.

There are some sign messages that are prescribed by federal or state regulations, so that the sign designer has little choice of what to convey to a user. In such cases, compliance is the only choice. The areas of pharmaceuticals, chemicals, and transportation of hazardous materials are examples of industries governed by strict sign prescriptives.

Other signs often require additional means to identify an exposure or hazard, usually markings. A good example is the highway sign "NO PASSING" (used on two-lane roads) in combination with a solid yellow line down the center of the roadway. Another example is that in the workplace it is common practice to use a sign that reads "CAUTION: DO NOT STACK MATERIALS IN AISLES" and then delineate the aisles (preferably) by using the combination of safety black with safety yellow lines.

The recently approved ASTM F1346, "Specifications for Safety Covers and Labeling Requirements for All Covers for Swimming Pools, Spas, and Hot Tubs,"[5] creates categories for each cover type as well as test methods and criteria for the same. A cover that is not a safety cover would normally have to comply only with the labeling section of the standard. An innovative approach introduced by this standard is a chart for manufacturers to identify any applicable hazards and then use the appropriate warning. A partial sample of how this chart applies is shown in Figure 13.

If this Hazard Exists	Add this Warning Statement
Will not support weight (as defined in this specification)	Stay off cover—will not support weight
Nonsecured or improperly secured covers	Keep children away
Concealment by slipping under cover	Children or objects cannot be seen under cover
Drowning on top of cover in accumulated surface water (as defined in this specification)	Remove standing water—child can drown on top of cover
Concealment, Entrapment— Drowning under cover	Remove cover(s) before entry of bathers—entrapment possible

Figure 13. Chart of hazards and appropriate warning statements from ASTM F1346, "Specifications for Safety Covers and Labeling Requirements for All Covers for Swimming Pools, Spas, and Hot Tubs."

Frequently, the question of space and placement of warnings signs is a multi-group concern (engineering vs. graphics vs. marketing), particularly where limited space is available. Product identification and performance characteristics often dictate what space is left for warnings. A study of large product liability claims[6] found that not complying with or not observing a product's warning or use label contributed to the accident in more than a quarter of the claims. Some product manufacturers opt for warnings on packaging. However, they often fail to consider that the package is usually discarded and a possible second user may not see the warning, if the primary warning is not on the product.

Hopefully, this chapter has provided a clear presentation of some of the pitfalls sign designers have created for themselves and have had to overcome. Warnings signs may seem complex and confusing, but concerted efforts at good signing should result in the ultimate objective: accident avoidance and injury mitigation.

CONSIDERATIONS FOR MORE EFFECTIVE SIGNS, LABELS, AND MARKINGS

In the event a hazard cannot be eliminated or guarded, a visual hazard alerting message should be used to inform the unwary, not only of the hazard but also of the degree of hazard and of appropriate actions to take to avoid accidents or their consequences. The very nature of precautionary warnings of potential hazards would require the use of standard formats, viewing distances, colors, shapes, and a clear understanding of the degree of hazard involved. A system which represents a uniform and consistent approach to the design of safety signs, labels, and tags is, therefore, essential.

A novice might ask: what is a safety sign? In short it is a visual alerting device which may take the form of a sign, label, tag, decal, marking, or placard, which essentially advises an observer of the nature and degree of a potential hazard which can cause injury, death or property damage. It may also provide precautions or evasive actions, information about consequences of ignoring the warning, or other directions to eliminate or reduce the hazard. In addition, a label/marking may refer someone to further information or instructions which would be too lengthy to place on a sign. Requirements for effective signs, labels, tags, or markings on products, in facilities, or any place in the environment must apply to all methods of manufacturing such devices. These include: etched, molded, die-stamped, paint-stenciled, burned, silk screened, indelibly stamped, or however manufactured.

CLASSES OF SIGNS, LABELS, AND TAGS

A very common way of categorizing signs/label/tags is by the signal word which, in essence, designates the exposure or level of hazard someone faces in a hazardous situation. The choice of a

proper signal word should be in consideration of acceptable definitions which specifically detail their application. Of course, when
federal, state, or local government codes, regulations, or standards
apply, the signal words mandated should be used.

If there is more than one hazard involved, one safety sign may
be used as long as the information provided covers each hazard
and a location is available which places the sign in close proxmity
to the hazards. Any signal word used in multiple hazard situations should address the level of greatest hazard. The signal word
or words used in safety alerting should always be located in a distinctive panel which is placed in the upper portion of the sign.

Classes of signs are established through the use of specific definitions, similar to the first definitions used in the Z35.1-1941 section on "Sign Purposes." These definitions have been revised and
are now a part of the Z535.2 and Z535.4 Standards.

Other Complementary Signs and Visual Alerting Devices

Notice and information signs are used to indicate a statement of
policy relating directly (or indirectly) to the safety of personnel or
protection of property, and other related markings in and around
the environment and/or product. Two "NOTICE" signs are shown
in Fig. 14. This signal word should not be associated directly with
a hazard or hazardous situation and must not be used in place of
"DANGER", "WARNING", or "CAUTION".

Figure 14. Two examples of "Notice" signs.

General safety signs, such as "Safety First", "Be Careful", or
"Think" (examples of which are shown in Fig. 15), require legends
which indicate general instructions relative to safe work practices,
reminders of proper safety procedures, and the locations of safety
equipment.

Figure. 15. Examples of general safety signs.

Fire Safety signs (such as those shown in Fig. 16) are used to indicate the location of emergency fire fighting equipment. (These signs indicate the location of equipment, etc., and not the direction to such equipment, etc.)

Figure 16. Examples of Fire Safety signs.

Directional arrow signs (shown in Fig. 17) are used to indicate the direction to entrances, exits, emergency equipment, safety equipment, directional movement of equipment or equipment functions and other locations important to safety.

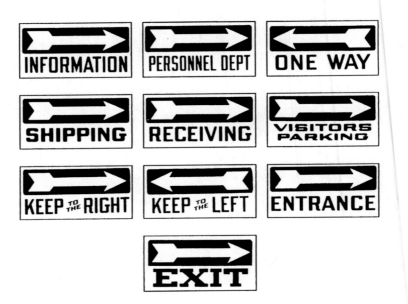

Figure 17. Examples of directional arrow signs.

Significantly, the "NOTICE" or "SAFETY INFORMATION" signs are not part of what might be termed "warning devices." However, these signs do provide vital information such as capacity ratings, sizes, types of products, etc., all of which relate to safe practices or procedures. There is often a tendency to information overload in this second tier of signs which can mitigate against sign effectiveness. In communication theory it has been concluded that the majority of people can only recall five to nine written items found in a series.[1] Quite obviously then, where detailed safety information is needed, detailed instruction manuals and training are essential.

SIGN CONFIGURATION

Signs, labels and tags have three basic configurations: one panel, two panels, or three panels. A one-panel sign (Figure 18) can have a signal word, a message, or a symbol/pictorial. (For more information about these signs consult ISO Recommendation No. 3864, "Safety Colours and Safety Signs.") A two-panel sign (Figure 19) has combinations of signal word, message, and symbol/pictorial.

The three-panel sign (Figure 20) uses all three combinations. Most importantly in two- and three-panel signs the signal word has top panel priority over the others used.

Figure 18. Examples of one-panel signs.

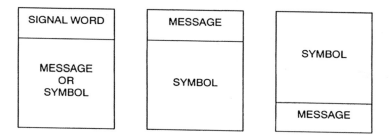

Figure 19. Examples of two-panel signs.

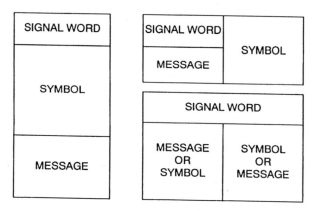

Figure 20. Examples of three-panel signs.

The increasing use of pictorials on signs to more clearly illustrate a hazard has led to greater use of three-panel signs. Pictorials, such as Figure 21, are also designed and used for some groups who have trouble reading printed messages.

Figure 21. An example of a pictorial used in a ladder marking.

A special geometric configuration around a symbol/pictorial is known as a "surround" or "surround shape." An example is the hazard alerting equilateral triangle or diamond placed around a symbol or pictorial. A red circle or circle with a diagonal slash over a pictorial or symbol of a smoking cigarette is another example, shown in Figure 22.

Figure 22. Example of a "surround" used in a "No-Smoking" sign.

Several other considerations important to sign development include: color, contrast, borders, symbols and pictorials, lettering, and placement.

Colors are important for the quick identification aspects of signs, but are only one component of such identification. However, it is not enough to simply require red, yellow, blue, green, etc. Studies have shown that the human eye does well at color matching or seeing small color differences; human color memory is, however, not very reliable. Therefore color standards or coding of the right color for a specific task is necessary. Safety colors should conform to the American National Standard Safety Color Code,

ANSI Z535.1-1991, which includes opaque and fluorescent colors, while reflective colors should conform to those specified in Federal Specification FP-79.

Contrast is the use of colors to achieve a desired state of color differentiation. Although black and blue may make beautiful combinations in the fashion world, they simply do not belong together on a sign where one is the message and the other is the background. Black on white, for greatest contrast, are probably the most used combinations. Some designs have used white letters on a black field or background. Others have used silver printing on black. "EXIT" signs are often found with red letters on a white lighted background, and with white letters on a red lighted background. Some jurisdictions mandate the green and white combination for EXITS. Contrast colors for signs become even more important in facilities with the currently fashionable muted pastel colors used for interior decoration and furnishings.

Borders also complement color because any border provides distinctive color contrast. Surround/surround shapes which outline signal words, symbols or pictorials should also be "bordered." Normally, where one color is used for the background, the same color used for the message or symbol/pictorial is used for the border. When more than two colors are used, experienced sign designers often bring their creativity to bear in designing a border, such as the one in Figure 23.

HAZARDOUS WASTE
FEDERAL LAW PROHIBITS IMPROPER DISPOSAL.
IF FOUND CONTACT THE NEAREST POLICE
PUBLIC SAFETY AUTHORITY OR THE
U.S. ENVIRONMENTAL PROTECTION AGENCY.
GENERATOR INFORMATION:
NAME
ADDRESS
CITY   STATE   ZIP
EPA   EPA
ID NO.   WASTE NO.
ACCUMULATION   MANIFEST
START DATE   DOCUMENT NO.

D.O.T. PROPER SHIPPING NAME AND UN OR NA NO. WITH PREFIX
HANDLE WITH CARE!

Figure 23. Illustration of a border designed to heighten the impact of a hazardous waste sign.

Symbols and pictorials usually clarify, supplement or are used to directly convey the message of a sign. When symbols are used, the panel on which they are presented should be square in shape. As indicated earlier, the intended message of a symbol or pictorial is to describe the nature of any hazard, potential consequences of such hazard, and/or any actions needed to avoid or evade the hazard. If any evaluation of a symbol is necessary, it should be in accordance with ANSI Z535.3-1991 "Criteria for Safety Symbols."

One of the first rules related to lettering size and style is "keep the message as concise as possible." The overall size of lettering is obviously determined by the length of the message and the distance from which the message must be easily read. Generally, letters should be sans serif style with signal words using capital or upper case only, while the message can be the same or a combination of upper and lower case.

Safe viewing distance of signal words requires the need to provide a reasonable hazard avoidance reaction time. The safe viewing distance for a message may vary according to, among other things, the size of the symbol or pictorial, level of lighting, and operation of equipment. Balance and legibility of a sign, in turn, is dependent on the combination of signal word, message length, and size of the symbol or pictorial used. For specific information on letter size and viewing distance, see ANSI Z535.4-1991, Annex A.[2]

Sign placement has some very simple rules. A sign must be seen, legible, clean, nondistracting (no visual noise around it), and not a hazard by its location. It should also be placed in the immediate vicinity of the identified hazard. A sign should not be easily removed or made ineffective; and, as much as possible, a sign should be placed so that it is protected against abrasion, damage, chemicals, ultra-violet light, or effects of weathering.

Development of Instruction Manuals as Complements to Signs

In a highly technological society, people do not understand how many things work, how they are made, what to look for, or what to avoid. This absence of knowledge is the reason for instruction manuals. Although most instruction manuals are usually for so called "end-user" products, they may also be found within a facility that designs its own products and processes for specialized use. Instruction manuals can take many forms, such as a detailed book, a multipage pamphlet, a one-page data sheet, or an instructional tag on a hand tool. Figure 24 is an example of the type and format of information presented in equipment manuals.

Specific precautions can be made more effective if they are set apart from routine instructions. This can be accomplished by using different colors or sizes of type or by placing the message in boldfaced type, boxed-in paragraphs or statements. Another good idea is to duplicate any safety sign in the text of a manual just as it appears on a machine, product or other equipment.

Manuals that accompany products or systems often include information on shipping/handling/storage, installation, operation, maintenance, service, or repair. In-house manuals are also often just as detailed. No matter what the purpose of manuals, it is essential that the information provided is meaningful and precise. Some of the more important considerations in the development of instruction manuals are:

- Can a product or process injure someone through normal use or from misuse?

- Is general safety information advisable and, if so, is it prominently displayed at the front of the manual?

- Is the product or process of such complexity for the typical user or operator that a sign/label/marking be put on a complicated product or process referring the user/operator to the instruction literature?

- Are instructions given for the replacement of worn or illegible signs/decals?

- Are any hazardous substances present in the product or process?

- Is there a need for capacity ratings, limits, or methods of lifting to be clearly spelled out?

- Are there any warnings on the importance of specific maintenance operations?

- Should only specially trained workers make certain adjustments or repairs to specific parts or equipment?

- Should cautions about typical "reasonably foreseeable misuse" be included?

The objective of any instruction manual should be to inform and give guidance to the operator for the safe operation and proper use of equipment.* A manual must never provide information just for the sake of marketing or sales, especially if it is misleading. Similarly, while advertisements should not show improper use of equipment, such as motorized equipment being driven up a 60° slope, this typical "reasonably foreseeable misuse" should be included, in instruction manuals. Merely giving orders/directions without including procedural instructions on how to implement the order should be avoided.

Special attention should be give to terminology and language when writing manuals, since readers must know precisely what is meant. A point may be clear to a writer with an engineering background, but not to the intended readers who operate a machine or a tool. Also, inaccurate use of special terms, may induce an unwarranted and unsafe sense of assurance on the part of user/readers.

---

*As an example, see ASTM F486.82, "Standard Recommended Practice for Preparation of Use and Care Booklets for Vacuum Cleaners."

SAFETY INSTRUCTIONS
WARNING

When using this equipment, basic safety precautions should always be followed to reduce the risk of fire, electrical shock, and personal injury. Failure to follow these instructions can result in severe personal injury.

READ ALL INSTRUCTIONS

GENERAL SAFETY CONSIDERATIONS

1. Before using equipment become familiar with all operating equipment.

2. Don't use equipment for unintended purposes.

3. Use safety glasses.

4. Keep work area clean and well illuminated. Dark, cluttered work areas and benches invite injuries.

5. Dress properly. Never operate the equipment while wearing loose clothes or jewelry. They can get caught in moving parts.

6. Stay alert. Do not operate equipment when tired.

7. Watch what you are doing at all times.

SPECIAL SAFETY PROCEDURES FOR EQUIPMENT

1. Guard against electric shock. Never operate equipment in damp or wet conditions.

2. Never operate equipment in presence of flammable liquids or gases.

3. All visitors should be kept away from work area when equipment is being operated.

4. Do not abuse the equipment.

5. Always lock out electric current from the equipment when performing maintenance.

6. Inspect equipment daily. If damaged, have proper personnel repair it.

7. Check for guards (condition and proper placement).

8. When servicing equipment, follow recommended procedures or get help.

Figure 24. Example of the type of information which may be presented in instruction manuals.

Citing applicable codes and standards or other specifications which govern the installation or operation of a product or process is essential. Be concise and to the point.

On the other hand, too often there are directions in electrical equipment manuals which simply state, "Follow all national, state, and local codes." This all inclusive statement is obviously deficient. When a code does specify certain requirements, the code should be followed. The best written and diagramed manuals should show a "typical safe installation" with service entrance requirements including voltage, amperage, wire size, plus wiring connections, color coding, grounding, etc., and also lockouts.

Where teamwork is an essential part of an operation, the message must be communicated to all concerned. To illustrate this, consider the teamwork necessary to launch a space shuttle. Not only do the astronauts in the shuttle need to know their roles, but also the personnel at the launch site, as well as at the control center far removed in Houston, Texas. Another example is the teamwork needed in changing dies on a large power press where various trades service the machinery.

If hazardous materials, such as toxic or flammable solvents, are recommended for operation and/or maintenance of a product or process, then appropriate guidance should be given covering related hazards.

Operating instructions should be as clear and concise as possible. Annotated pictures of equipment within a facility, rather than simulated diagrams or drawings, will minimize confusion where special parts or controls must be identified. When parts are listed, it is critical to identify safety components and to use "exploded views" (such as Fig. 25) showing placement and/or function within a product or process.

All illustrations should show proper guards in place on machines and correctly adjusted for use. Operators, if shown, should be wearing appropriate clothing and protective equipment. When an illustration must show equipment without guards, specific information must be given, for example:

DANGER: HAZARDOUS MOVING PARTS.
Cover guards removed for illustration only.
DO NOT OPERATE WITH ANY GUARDS REMOVED!

Similarly, many times manuals require electrical lockout for maintenance or repair; however, in some instances adjustments must be made with power on (electricity and/or hydraulics). In such cases, special precautions must be written to advise workers of the hazards.

To minimize confusion and the possibility of overlooking instructions, the composition of a manual should be such that each subject (installation, operation, maintenance, etc.) is kept within respective sections and not divided throughout the manual. Completeness and adequacy of detail concerning each subject is essential. Specific safety warnings should be inserted at the point

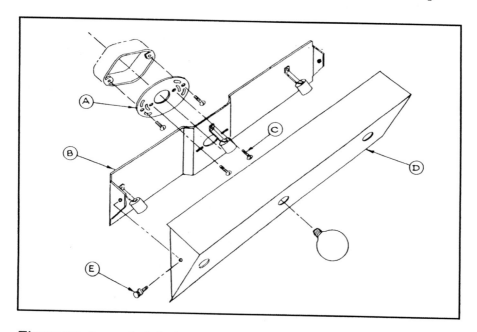

Figure 25. An exploded view of a light fixture.

in the description or instruction where they apply. Such treatment emphasizes the safe method as an integral part of the operation. It may also be highly desirable to provide a special general safety section at the beginning of the manual.

Some manual writers will select an arbitrary symbol, such as the one shown in Figure 26, and present this symbol as a warning of potential injury. By defining such at the start of the manual, the symbol only may be subsequently used. Similarly, where there is the potential of damage to machinery, an arbitrary symbol may be defined and subsequently only the symbol utilized.

Figure 26. An example of one possible "arbitrary symbol" that might be used in manuals when warning of potential injury.

Improvements or changes in a product or process can alter safety characteristics. When modification data is released, the compatibility of the original modifications to the original instruction manual should be carefully considered. If a manual was issued as a loose-leaf binder, replacement pages can be developed following carefully worded accompanying instructions on how to update the manual. Bound manuals can be updated using stick-on (self-adhesive) partial-page corrections, in lieu of replacing the entire publication. When a publication is replaced, user's should be advised to destroy old copies or take them out of the distribution chain. Updates to manuals with tables of contents should identify revised portions and dates of revisions in the preface.

There are several important factors to consider when deciding to use a warning in instruction manuals. Among these factors are:

(1) *Hidden Hazards*— When someone might not be aware of the presence of a hazard.

DANGER

High voltage is present at contacts of hydraulic pressure switch.

(2) *Obvious Hazards*—
Usually a reminder of something a person would likely take for granted.

WARNING

Personal Injury Hazard

Avoid opening dishwasher door before dishwasher is installed. Dishwasher, before it is installed, may tip over when door is opened, resulting in personal injury or product damage.

(3) *Reasonable Misuse*—
This term suggests the need to warn of a hazard's consequences prior to doing something wrong.

WARNING

Electrical Shock Hazard

Disconnect power before making electrical connection. Failure to do so could result in electrical shock.

(4) *Associated Hazards*—
Where hazards exist simply because of special work performed or materials used.

CAUTION

Product Damage

- **Protect dishwasher and water lines leading to dishwasher against freezing.**
- **Do Not use plastic pipe.**

Failure to do so could cause inlet valve, water lines leading to dishwasher, water lines in dishwasher and drain to rupture.

As indicated previously, instruction manuals should be designed to ensure the continued safe operation of equipment and processes and to minimize the consequences of any failure which might cause an accident. From a liability aspect, a sound practice is to obtain a written receipt or other appropriate steps, verifying that a manual was delivered to a user. Obviously, the instruction manual is not the total answer by itself. There should be a method or procedure through periodic training to ensure that readers/users know the importance of the manual and that it does not just gather dust on an office bookshelf. Provision should be made to ensure that instruction manuals are readily available. The manual can be marked appropriately to remind users of its importance. In addition, a sign or label can be affixed to a product and/or packaging, or conveniently located in a process area, directing the user or operator to read and understand the manual. If there is sufficient space in proximity to the operator's station, a shelf, drawer, or chain can be used to attach the manual to the machinery or otherwise make sure it is accessible. All these considerations should help to achieve the desired objective of manuals.

A UNIFORM GUIDE TO SIGN DEVELOPMENT—

SOME CONSIDERATIONS FOR A SYSTEMATIC AND UNIFORM APPROACH WHEN DESIGNING SIGNS/LABELS/MARKINGS

- A systematic approach is needed to address all contingencies of design, construction, application, use, and placement of signs. Is everything covered?

- Awareness of research and other governmental codes and private sector standards is useful to ascertain the parameters of the system. Does a government standard specify, for example, signal word or color?

- The system should minimize the number of design formats and layouts while allowing flexibility to meet individual users' needs and situations.

- The system should address the number of ways signs can be applied or manufactured, that is, die-stamped, stenciled, burned into materials, etc.

- The design/format of non-vehicular signs, for products, facilities, or other hazardous situations is generally a two-panel (upper for signal word and lower for precautionary action/or re-enforcing emphasis) rectangular arrangement or layout. However, pictorial and symbol panels can be used (square in shape) to clarify, supplement, or substitute for the worded message in the lower action-emphasis panel.

- Ideally, signs may employ a signal word, name of hazard, avoidance activity, and consequences of failing to take action. However, if the hazards are known and recognized by the targeted viewers, the signs need not carry the consequences and action avoidance messages. (For selection of an appropriate signal word see the definitions in the Z535 series.)

- Hazards should provide information which addresses specific injury situations, property damage or both, the elements of accidents and injuries.

- The key to a balanced and legible sign format is to provide a safe viewing distance which permits a reasonable hazard avoidance reaction time.

- After determining signal word (sans serif upper case only), message length (sans serif only; upper/lower case combination) and, if used, the size of the symbol, the letter size can be calculated which will provide maximum readability consistent with safe viewing distance— a distance determined to provide sufficient hazard avoidance reaction time.

- A very concise message should be crafted so that the largest letter size will permit a safe viewing distance.

- Research and reference sources used as rationale for selecting elements of the sign system should be relevant and not chosen for public relations purposes or erudition.

- It is critical place a sign in the immediate vicinity of the hazard. Failing to do so could lessen or even eliminate the safety impact of even the best designed sign.

NOTES

CHAPTER 2: EXPLORING THE PROBLEMS OF SIGNS

1. Ralph L. Barnett and Dennis Brinkman, "Safety Hierarchy," *Safety Brief*, vol.3, no.2 (Niles, Illinois: Triodyne Inc., June 1985).

2. *Webster's New World Dictionary*, Second College Edition (Englewood Cliffs, New Jersey: William Collins World Publishing Co., Inc., Prentice-Hall, Inc., 1991).

3. "Guidelines for the Inclusion of Safety Aspects in Standards," *ISO/IEC Guide 51*, Sec. 3.1, Note 1, (Geneva: International Organization for Standardization, 1990).

CHAPTER 3: DEVELOPMENT AND HISTORY OF SIGN STANDARDIZATION

1. American National Standard, "Specifications for Industrial Accident Prevention Signs," ASA Z35.1-1941 (New York: American Standards Association [now the American National Standards Institute]).

2. M.G. Moore, "Product Warning Effectiveness," *Professional Safety*, vol. 36, no.4 (April 1991), pp. 21-24.

3. American National Standard, "Specifications for Accident Prevention Signs," ANSI Z35.1-1972 (New York: American National Standards Institute).

4. American National Standard, "Specifications for Informational Signs Complementary to ANSI Z35.1-1972, Accident Prevention Signs," ANSI Z35.4-1973 (New York: American National Standards Institute).

5. American National Standard, "Precautionary Labeling of Hazardous Industrial Chemicals," ANSI Z129-1988 (New York: American National Standards Institute).

6. American National Standard, "Safety Color Code for Marking Physical Hazards," ANSI Z53.1-1979, (New York: American National Standards Institute).

7. American National Standards: "Safety Color Code," ANSI Z535.1-1991; "Environmental and Facility Signs," ANSI Z535.2-1991; "Criteria for Safety Symbols," ANSI Z535.3-1991; "Product Safety Signs and Labels," ANSI Z5235.4-1991; "Accident Prevention Tags," ANSI Z535.5-1991 (Washington, D.C.: National Electrical Manufacturers Association).

CHAPTER 4: THE ROLE OF RESEARCH IN DEVELOPING SIGNS

1. Thomas F. Bresnahan, "Hazard Association Value of Safety Signs," *Professional Safety,* vol. 30, no. 7, (July, 1985), pp. 26-31.

2. *A14 Ladder Standard Rationale Statement* (Chicago: American Ladder Institute, 1982).

3. B.L. Collins and N.D. Lerner, "Assessment of Fire-Safety Symbols," *Human Factors,* 24:1, (1982), pp. 75-84.

CHAPTER 5: LEGAL IMPLICATIONS

1. Harry M. Philo, "New Dimensions in the Tortious Failure to Warn," *Professional Safety,* vol. 27, no. 11 (November 1982), pp. 23-29.

CHAPTER 6: CURRENT PRACTICES AND USAGE OF SIGNS, LABELS, AND MARKINGS

1. American National Standard Z535.1-1991, "Safety Color Code" (New York: American National Standards Institute).

2. M.S. Wogalter, S.W. Jarrard, and S.N. Simpson, "Effects of Warning Signal Words on Hazard Perceptions of Consumer Products," *Proceedings of the Human Factors Society's 36th Annual Meeting*, October 12-16, 1992, Atlanta, Georgia.

3. American National Standard Z535.3, "Criteria for Safety Symbols," (New York: American National Standards Institute).

4. J.P. Frantz, J.M., Miller, M.R. Lehto, "Must the context be considered when applying generic safety symbols?: A case study in flammable contact adhesives." *Journal of Safety Research*, vol.22, no. 3 (Chicago: National Safety Council, 1991), pp. 147-61.

5. ASTM F1346, "Specifications for Safety Covers for Swimming Pools, Spas, and Hot Tubs" (Philadelphia: ASTM).

6. Alliance of American Insurers, *Large Product Liability Claims Study* (1985), Schaumburg, IL.

CHAPTER 7: CONSIDERATIONS FOR MORE EFFECTIVE SIGNS, LABELS, AND MARKINGS

1. George A. Miller, "The Magical Number Seven, Plus or Minus Two," The Psychological Review, vol 63, no. 2 (March 1956), p. 81-97.

2. American National Standard, "Product Safety Signs and Labels," ANSI Z535.4-1991 (Washington, D.C.: National Electric Manufacturers Association).

GLOSSARY

Absolute Liability

When the producer or seller is held strictly liable for a defective product, regardless of the care exercised in its manufacture, the only proof required by the injured party is a casual connection between his injury and the product.

Acceptable Level of Risk

The residual risk after safeguarding is applied while keeping machinery, products or processes in proper working order.

Accident

An unplanned event which interrupts the completion of an activity, and may or may not include property damage or injury.

American National Standards Institute (ANSI)

A non-profit organization, dedicated to the preparation and publication of safety standards for manufacturers, contractors, consumers and the general public and serves as the clearinghouse and coordinating body for standards activity nationally, in the U.S.A. Normally, all standards must be reaffirmed or updated every five (5) year intervals.

Class Action

A suit brought by one or more named plaintiffs who seek compensation from a/an individual or individuals, corporation(s), municipality or a licensing/regulatory body for an injury or loss resulting from negligence or error. Just as the named plaintiffs may sue as representatives of a class, the named defendants may be sued as representatives of a class of unnamed defendants who are alleged to be similarly at fault.

Contract

An agreement, usually in writing, between two parties in which a producer, seller or service provider agrees that his/her product or services will perform certain functions and outlines the intended and expected use of the product or services. Contractors may extend further and encompass further agreements, commonly referred to as Indemnity Agreements, Hold-Harmless Agreements, etc., which can impose additional liabilities on the manufacturer, seller or service provider than would be imposed upon him/her by common law, unless prohibited by law. A verbal contract may be binding, provided that the parties agree on the terms, and are willing to abide by them.

Critical Parts

Those components that affect the safety of a product for its intended life.

Damage

The alteration of the utility of machinery or process(es).

Disclaimer

A specific denial of responsibility for liability arising out of services performed, or improperly performed, or not performed; or arising out of a product or the use thereof. Ultimately the extent of enforceability of a disclaimer is determined by the court.

Discovery

Investigation into the facts of a claim and/or the alleged proximate cause of injury. Discovery may include interrogatories, depositions, expert examination of the product in question, plaintiff's medical history, etc.

Deposition

The taking of pertinent testimony, not in court, but under oath in the presence of attorneys for the plaintiff and the defendant. The deposed person may be anyone having knowledge of the plaintiff's injury or the allegedly defective product in question.

Exposure

A situation where the risk of an accident is imminent to an individual, machinery, product or process.

Hazard

A real or potential condition or characteristic of a material, product, or process that presents a risk of injury and/or damage to property. Examples are an unguarded machine or tool; a hazardous or toxic chemical; or, a forklift truck without overhead guard.

Hold-Harmless Agreements

A contract under which the legal liability, in whole or in part, of one party for damages is waived under terms of the agreement. (See: Contract; Disclaimer.)

International Organization for Standardization (ISO), Geneva, Switzerland

Like ANSI, the ISO is dedicated to the preparation and publication of safety standards for manufacturers, contractors, consumers and the public and serves as the clearing house and coordinating body for standards worldwide.

Interrogatories

A series of formal written questions propounded by either party to a legal action and served on the adversary for the purpose of discovery. The questions must be pertinent to the case and must be answered, except where objected to by counsel for legal cause. Such questions and answers are normally filed with the trial court. These can be used at the trial, especially for impeachment purposes.

Issues, External and Internal

External issues are those that bear upon sign design and development relating to: the effectiveness or adequacy of the message communicated, the need to protect the user, and requirements for and to provide warnings. Internal issues are those related to standardization of sign design and placement, and which specific audiences are targeted.

Liability

The state of being bound or obliged by law to do, pay or make good something; includes the law of torts, which is usually based on legal decisions involving negligence.

Negligence

The failure to do something which a "reasonable person" would do, or the doing of something which a reasonable and prudent person would not do. This includes the reasonableness of a manufacturer's action in designing and selling products. Increasingly, litigation on products are brought on the theory of strict liability in tort, breach of warranty, failure to warn, etc., and fewer cases on the difficult to prove allegation of negligence.

OSHA

Abbreviation for the Occupational Safety and Health Administration, a federal agency set up by the U.S. Congress, under the Department of Labor, through the enactment of the Occupational Safety and Health Act of 1970. Its main function is to establish and enforce standards related to safety and health in the workplace.

Panel

The area within a safety sign which is differentiated from other areas by a line, border, margin or background color. A maximum of three (3) panels are allowed per sign:

(1) Signal Word Panel
(2) Message Panel
(3) Symbol/Pictorial Panel

Privity of Contract

Often referred to as merely "Privity," the term originated with early interpretations of contractual law to the effect that the benefits or detriments within the contract applied only to the parties named in the contract and would not inure to the benefit or detriment to any other parties. Lack of privity had been an absolute defense for the seller or manufacturer in a claim for breach of warrant. Over the years, this defense has slowly been eroded and is now permitted as a defense in only a few states. In the majority of states breach of warranty is breach of contract, expressed or implied.

Product Liability

The responsibility of a manufacturer or seller to the purchaser or user of its product(s) for injury or damage resulting from negligence or breach of warranty in their manufacture, sale, handling, or distribution, or if the product(s) is/are more hazardous than is normal for other, similar products. A manufacturer can also be held liable for defective materials, imprudent design, absence of proper signs/labels or instructions, or failure to provide safeguards.

Sign/Label/Marking

Are those communications devices used to alert users/readers/viewers to an anticipated risk of injury or hazard imminent in the environment/facility or use of a product or system.

Signal Word

A communication device, usually one word, used to indicate the degree or level of safety alert or hazard. These are:

(1) DANGER
(2) WARNING
(3) CAUTION
(4) NOTICE

General safety signs employ one or more signal words such as "Be Careful," "Safety First," "Think," etc. They are used to give instructions on safe work practices or procedures and location of equipment.

State of the Art

Applicable technology or design criteria known by, or available to, a manufacture at the time a particular product was manufactured.

Statute of Limitations

Each state statutorily imposes a time limitation on a plaintiff within which a pending court action must be filed. This varies by state, but is generally longer for a contract action than for negligence. In one state, a person who is injured and bases his/her action on negligence must file suit within two years of the date of the alleged injury, or s/he is barred from filing legal action. If the action is based on contract, the limitation is six years. A Breach of Warranty action falls in the latter category. Many states extend the time limits by saying the statue of limitations period starts when the injured party first discovers a probability of a casual connection between his injury and a product, even through the connection may only become suspect years after the initial injury.

Statute of Repose

The period of elapsed time, as defined by state statutes, from the date a product is manufactured or first sold to a user, during which a user can sue claiming injury by the product. In those relatively few states that have such a statute, the time limits vary from six to twelve years. However, various statutes may provide for an extended period under certain extenuating circumstances.

Strict Liability

If a product is used as intended, and the consumer is injured due to defect the manufacturer is held strictly liable for damages regardless of the care exercised in selling and/or manufacturing the product. Liability will be imposed no mater how careful the manufacturer was in design, quality control and production, if the court finds the condition presented by the product to be unreasonably dangerous. In simple terms, the burden of proof of blame or fault has been removed from the plaintiff.

Surround or Surround Shape

A geometric figure around a symbol or pictorial used to provide added information or emphasis by its configuration.

Symbol or Pictorial

The use of a graphic presentation to communicate a message without using words. A symbol pictorial may be one or a combination of the following: a specific hazard; a hazardous situation; a precaution to take to avoid the hazard; or, the result when the hazard cannot be avoided.

Unsafe Act

An exposure to a hazard or a failure to adhere to established rules, regulations, practices, or procedures.

Unsafe Condition

A physical state in which a hazard is created which may cause an accident.

REFERENCES

American National Standard Institute. *Safety Color Code,* Z535.1. New York, 1991.

——. *Environmental and Facility Signs,* Z535.2. New York, 1991.

——. *Criteria for Safety Symbols,* Z535.3. New York, 1991.

——. *Product Safety Signs and Labels,* Z535.4. New York, 1991.

——. *Accident Prevention Tags,* Z535.5. New York, 1991.

American Society for Testing and Materials. *Annual Book of ASTM Standards.* Philadelphia, 1991.

——. *Practice for Preparation of Use and Care Booklets for Vacuum Cleaners,* F486-87, Philadelphia, 1987.

Bass, Lewis. *Products Liability: Design and Manufacturing Defects.* Colorado Springs, Colorado: Shepard's/McGraw Hill, 1986.

Bresnahan, Thomas F., and Bryk, Joseph. "Hazard Association Values of Accident Prevention Signs." *Professional Safety* 20 (March 1975), no.3.

Canavan, Michael M. *Product Liability for Supervisors and Managers.* Reston, Virginia: Reston Publishing Company, Inc., 1981.

Freedman, Warren. *Products Liability: For Corporate Counsels, Controllers, and Product Safety Executives.* New York: Van Nostrand Reinhold Company, 1984.

Hammer, Willie. *Product Safety Management and Engineering.* 2 ed. Des Plaines, Illinois: American Society of Safety Engineers, 1993.

Lehto, Mark R., and Miller, James M. *WARNINGS: Fundamentals, Design, and Evaluation Methodologies.* Vol. 1. Ann Arbor, Michigan: Fuller Technical Publications, 1990.

Lehto, Mark R., Miller, James M.; and Frantz, J. Paul. *Instructions and Warnings: The Annotated Bibliography.* Ann Arbor, Michigan: Fuller Technical Publications, 1990.

National Safety Council. *Product Safety Management Guidelines.* Chicago, 1989.

Seiden, R. Mathiew. *Product Safety Engineering for Managers: A Practical Handbook and Guide.* Englewood, New Jersey: Prentice-Hall, Inc., 1984.

Standards for Safety Annual Catalog. Northbrook, Illinois: Underwriters Laboratories, Inc.

Triodyne Safety Briefs. "On Classification of Safeguard Devices (Part I)." vol.1, no.1. Niles, Illinois: Triodyne, Inc., April 1981.

——. "On Classification of Safeguard Devices (Part II)." vol.1, no.2. Niles, Illinois: Triodyne, Inc., Sept. 1981.

——. "Philosophical Aspects of Dangerous Safety Systems." vol.1, no.4. Niles, Illinois: Triodyne, Inc., Dec. 1982.

——. "Safety Hierarchy." vol.3, no.2. Niles, Illinois: Triodyne, Inc., June 1985.

——. "The Dependency Hypothesis (Part I)," vol.2, no.3. Niles, Illinois: Triodyne, Inc., Nov. 1983.

——. "The Dependency Hypothesis (Part II-Expected Use)," vol.3, no.1. Niles, Illinois: Triodyne, Inc., Dec. 1984.

Weinstein et al. *Products Liability and the Reasonably Safe Product.* New York: John Wiley and Sons, 1978.

INDEX

About the Authors—

Thomas F. Bresnahan, *CSP*

While Director of Safety Standards for the National Safety Council, Mr. Bresnahan served as Secretary of the American National Standards Z35 on Signs Symbols and Colors for six years. In his capacity as Secretary, he created surveys and various data collection instruments for assessing precautionary warning devices. His two research studies on the American National Standard Z35, as well as the ISO "Safety Colours and Safety Signs," were published in *Professional Safety* magazine. In addition, he served as chairman of the Visual Alerting Systems Committee of ANSI's Safety and Health Standards Board. As Secretary of the ANSI A14 Ladder Standards project, Mr. Bresnahan headed a Task Force to design a questionnaire for a field survey of consumers. He is a member of the American National Standard Z535 Committee, Signs, Symbols and Colors. In 1989 he was appointed Director of Technical Services for the American Society of Safety Engineers.

Donald C. Lhotka, *CSP*

As Administrator of Product Liability Prevention for the Borg-Warner Corporation in the 1980's, Mr. Lhotka's department developed product use and warning labels as well as installation and maintenance manuals for the company's fifty manufacturing facilities. In the 1970's, as Manager of Traffic Safety activities for the National Safety Council, he was involved in the development of the "Manual on Uniform Traffic Control Devices" (ANSI D6).

Harry Winchell, *P.E., CSP*

Mr. Winchell is a former Division Technical Director with Liberty Mutual Insurance Company. During his thirty-five year career with Liberty, he served in a number of administrative and technical positions, including responsibility for the evaluation of technical manuals. Mr. Winchell has held membership and officer positions in the National Fire Protection Association, National Safety Council, and did liaison work for the ASSE. He served on several NFPA and ANSI Standards committees including ANSI Z535, Safety Signs and Colors.